For Ellen Palestrant and Susan Pearson, sunshine on my garden –J. H.

For my dear friends Philippe and Liliane –C. D.

Text © 2006 by Juanita Havill.
Illustrations © 2006 by Christine Davenier.

Book design by Kristen M. Nobles and Kristine Brogno.
Typeset in Interlude and Optima.
The illustrations in this book were rendered in ink.
Manufactured in China.

Library of Congress Cataloging-in-Publication Data
Havill, Juanita.
I heard it from Alice Zucchini : poems about the garden /
by Juanita Havill ; illustrated by Christine Davenier.
p. cm.
ISBN-13: 978-0-8118-3962-4
ISBN-10: 0-8118-3962-1
1. Gardens—Juvenile poetry. 2. Gardening—Juvenile poetry. 3.
Children's poetry, American. I. Davenier, Christine, ill. II. Title.
PS3558.A784612 2005
2004013365

Distributed in Canada by Raincoast Books
9050 Shaughnessy Street
Vancouver, British Columbia V6P 6E5

10 9 8 7 6 5 4 3 2 1

Chronicle Books LLC
85 Second Street
San Francisco, California 94105

www.chroniclekids.com

I HEARD IT FROM
ALICE ZUCCHINI
POEMS ABOUT THE GARDEN

By Juanita Havill   Illustrated by Christine Davenier

chronicle books·san francisco

CONTENTS

WHEN I GROW UP 7

INSTRUCTIONS 8

SEEDLINGS 9

CUCUMBERS 9

THE MONSTER 10

SWEET CICELY AND THE BEE 12

LIGHT BULBS 12

PEA POD CHANT 13

NURSERY RHYME 14

BLUE MOON OVER THE GARDEN 15

SNAP BEANS 16

CARROTS 16

DAINTY DOILY DILL WEED 17

GARDEN GOSSIP 18

WHAT I LIKE ABOUT JULY 20

SUMMER STORM 21

THE PUMPKIN'S REVENGE 22

GARDEN LULLABY 24

VEGETABLE STEW 27

BURIED 28

WHEN I GROW UP

In the still chill of a winter night
seeds on the gardener's bench
rattle their packets
with chattering.

"When I grow up,
I'm going to be . . ."

"The biggest watermelon."
"Greenest spinach."
"Toughest kale."
"A rutabaga round as the world."
"An everywhere zucchini vine."
"Cornstalk so tall I touch the sky."

Little seeds
with big plans,
chittering, chattering,
except for one,
not a murmur from his packet.

Hey, little seed,
what about you?
What will you be
when you grow up?

In the still chill of the winter night:
"I'm going to be FIRST!"

And the radish is right.

INSTRUCTIONS

Plant seeds early in the spring
when the ground is warm,
two inches deep in well-tilled soil
where they'll be safe from harm.

Let the sun and rain pour down.
Be careful where you hoe.
A miracle is taking place:
Seeds split and start to grow.

SEEDLINGS

Weedling seedlings
sprout at night,
at dawn, at noon
in broad daylight.

Weedling seedlings
of all kinds—
crabgrass, vetch,
and tangling vines.

Weedling seedlings
choking out
pea-lings, bean-lings
as they sprout.

Weedling seedlings,
sneak attack.
Yank them out,
but they'll be back.

CUCUMBERS

There's something fishy in the garden,
lurking in the shadow of leaves.
What waits shivering,
unknown, unnamed,
as the midnight fisher
reels in the vine
and counts his catch—
one by one—
in the ripple of moonlight?

THE MONSTER

There's a monster in the garden.
He's standing in the dirt
in a pair of ragged jeans
and a yellow flannel shirt.

A straw hat on his head.
His boots are full of holes.
Is he here to scare the grubs
or chase away the moles?

Whatever he is up to,
he's scared the pumpkins white.
Tomatoes cower on their vines
and celery shakes in fright.

Lettuce leaves are wilting.
Green beans scatter wide.
When news gets to the broccoli,
there's no place left to hide.

Nightmares haunt the vegetables,
sleepless in their bed,
but then two sparrows build a nest
atop the monster's head.

Veggies watch the sparrows hatch,
shouting, "Look at that!"
"You can't scare *us*, you monster, in
your silly, chirping hat."

SWEET CICELY AND THE BEE

On a morning in May
with dew on her face
Sweet Cicely looks up to see,
hovering above,
declaring his love,
an elegant gentleman bee.

"Oh, lovely sweet flower,
you have such power,
I cannot resist your perfume.
Will you be my wife
for the rest of my life?
Say yes or my life will be gloom."

"I would like to agree,"
says Sweet Cicely,
drawn to the buzz in his rhyme.
"But I flower in May,
in June, go away.
How could we have enough time?"

"We'll pretend that an hour
is a year, my sweet flower.
Let's marry today before three."
No happier pair
exists anywhere
than Sweet Cicely and the bee.

LIGHT BULBS

In the darkness under the garden,
how do worms know where to go?
They switch on the light bulb radishes
and crawl in the beams of their glow.

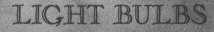

PEA POD CHANT

One pod, two pods, three pods, four.
Who's that knocking at the door?

Rat-a-tat rain, I've come to play.
Shivery raindrops, go away.

One pod, two pods, three pods, four.
Who's that whistling at the door?

Whoosh-a-whoosh wind, please let me in.
Not by the green of our skinny-skin-skin.

One pod, two pods, three pods, four.
Who's that beaming at the door?

Razz-a-dazz sun. No need to pout.
Yo! Mister Sun. We'll be right out.

NURSERY RHYME

In the Rhubarb Forest
lives the King of the Beetles,
wearing armor of golden green.
In safety and secrecy,
in comfort and splendor he
happily reigns with his Queen.

On a sunlit June morning
an axe-wielding giant
chops away with a menacing cry.
"Take that!" The Queen dies.
"Take that!" The King flies.
And the forest is baked in a pie.

BLUE MOON OVER THE GARDEN

A blue moon rising over the garden
ends the enchantment of a hundred years.
Sleeping vegetables wake and yawn.
It's June and the night of the second full moon.
Crickets tune their violins in anticipation.
Tomatoes bounce down pole-bean twine.
Cucumbers tumble in green clown suits.
A choir of celery bursts into song:
"Wake up, Princess, the time is now!"
At last she appears
and the dance begins.
Princess Asparagus sighs,
rubs her eyes,
then rises on her green-slippered toes
to waltz with her prince
in the blue moonlight.

GARDEN GOSSIP

I heard it from Alice Zucchini.
I wonder what the neighbors will say.
Max Bean said a bad word at recess,
so bad that Ms. Spinach turned gray.
Marge Sweet Pea threw up on the author
while he spoke in her classroom today.

I heard it from Alice Zucchini.
I wonder what the neighbors will say.
Jill Celery is up to her tricks:
ringing doorbells then running away.
Sam Melon is locked in the bathroom.
He's been there for more than a day.

I heard it from Alice Zucchini.
I don't know what the neighbors will do.
But I heard it from Alice Zucchini,
so I doubt if a word of it's true.

WHAT I LIKE
ABOUT JULY

Breezes combing the wavy tassels
of my hair,
the sparkle of my long green leaves
in the heat of the sun at noon,
the thrill of lightning,
the boom-boom beat of thunder.
But what I like most
about July
is growing
tall,
taller,
tallest,
and how everyone looks up to me.

SUMMER STORM

"Don't be afraid
of a summer storm.
Lay your little cauliflower head
next to mine."

"But, Mama, what is that big noise?"

"Giant purple cabbages
roughhousing in the sky."

"But, Mama, what is that flash of light?"

"Lightning bugs so high above the clouds
no rain will put them out."

"Oh, Mama, I think I'm getting scared."

"Don't be afraid
of a summer storm.
Look up and let the splash of raindrops
wash your face.
Then lay your little cauliflower head
next to mine
where you'll be safe.
You'll always be safe."

THE PUMPKIN'S REVENGE

"You're too pale." "You're too fat."
"Your creases aren't fine."
"Your stems are the grossest on the vine."

The ugly pumpkin weathered the taunts
of his nattering neighbors who tried to flaunt
their tidy stems, their bright orange skin,
until—one misty night in fall,
the evening of a royal ball,
the pumpkin farmer asleep in his shack,
a flash of light zapped the pumpkin patch.
In a puff of smoke and a shower of stars
stood a dinky fairy
with grandmother wrinkles and silver hair,
pacing the patch with a purposeful stare,
until—but then you know the story
of the scrub girl's journey from rags to glory,
of her dazzling clothes and crystal slippers,
her golden carriage and royal marriage,
her homely stepsisters' chubby heels
and overgrown toes.
What you heard is not true,
not every word.
If you're thinking the pumpkin
became compost or pie,
you're wrong. I'll tell you why.
The farmer who slept during magic at night
woke the third morning to the sight
of a shimmering carriage in his meager patch.
The ugly pumpkin, so heckled and shamed,
defied the fairy deadline and remained
a one-of-a-kind carriage in gilded frame.
You can see him today in a Paris museum.

The farmer got rich from the sale of the coach,
lived happily ever after with his wife,
homely stepsister of the princess bride.
He loved her, it is said,
big feet and all.

GARDEN LULLABY

Sudden hush when the sun goes down.
Night in the garden and the soothing sound
of crickets chirping lullabies.

Sweet dreams, little peas, ten to a pod.
Good night, radishes, tucked under sod.
Gone are the bees and butterflies.

Heads of lettuce wilted by sun
recuperate when the day is done.
Closed are all the potatoes' eyes.

Tomatoes snooze and eggplants doze.
All is still while the moonlight glows
save crickets chirping lullabies.

VEGETABLE STEW

Ra-ta-ta. Ra-ta-ta. Ra-ta-ta-too!
"We shall go dancing, and I'm taking you."
Tomato invited Sweet Pepper
to a club called the Vegetable Stew.

There Onion was simmering with Garlic
in a tango that took only two.
"Wow!" said Tomato to Eggplant.
"Watch what that onion can do."

The tune changed abruptly to hip-hop.
The zucchinis invaded the floor,
leaping, high-stepping, and spinning
until the crowd hollered for more.

Round midnight the band started swinging
and the Herb Girls appeared on the stage.
They harmonized, blended, and melded:
Parsley, Thyme, Bay Leaf, and Sage.

Tomato requested a slow dance.
Sweet Pepper was having a ball.
She whispered, "Next time you go dancing,
be sure to give me a call."

Ra-ta-ta. Ra-ta-ta. Ra-ta-ta-too.
We can't imagine a better venue—
the **hip-hoppest,**

        swingiest,

                spiciest,

                      liveliest nightclub,
THE VEGETABLE STEW!

BURIED

Brush aside fresh fallen snow.
Dig down deep where frost can't go.
Wrapped in brown from head to toe—
What do you know?—
A potato!